Insects
and
Spiders

Flies

Shane F McEvey
for the Australian Museum

This edition first published in 2002 in the United States of America by Chelsea House Publishers, a subsidiary of Haights Cross Communications.

Chelsea House Publishers
1974 Sproul Road, Suite 400
Broomall, PA 19008-0914

The Chelsea House world wide web address is www.chelseahouse.com

Library of Congress Cataloging-in-Publication Data Applied for.

ISBN 0-7910-6596-0

First published in 2001 by
Macmillan Education Australia Pty Ltd
627 Chapel Street, South Yarra, Australia, 3141

Edited by Anna Fern
Text design by Nina Sanadze
Cover design by Nina Sanadze
Australian Museum Publishing Unit: Jennifer Saunders and Catherine Lowe
Australian Museum Series Editor: Deborah White

Printed in China

Acknowledgements
Our thanks to Martyn Robinson, Max Moulds and Margaret Humphrey for helpful discussion and comments.

The author and the publisher are grateful to the following for permission to reproduce copyright material:

Cover: A papaya fruit fly, photo by Steve Wilson/Nature Focus.

Andrew Davoll/Lochman Transparencies, p. 15 (top); Australian Museum/Nature Focus, pp. 26 (bottom), 27;
C. Andrew Henley/Nature Focus, pp. 5 (top), 22 (top), 30; Carl Bento/Nature Focus, pp. 19 (bottom),
21 (bottom right); CSIRO Australia, p. 24; Dennis Sarson/Lochman Transparencies, pp. 17 (top), 26 (top);
E. E. Zillman/Nature Focus, p. 9; Geoff Avern/Nature Focus, p. 8 (middle); Howard Hughes/Nature Focus,
p. 28; Jiri Lochman/Lochman Transparencies, pp. 6–7 (all), 8 (top and bottom left), 10 (top), 11 (top and bottom),
12 (top), 13 (all), 15 (middle and bottom), 16 (top), 17 (bottom), 18 (top and bottom), 19 (top and middle),
20, 21 (top and bottom left), 22 (middle and bottom), 23 (all), 25 (top); Michael Cermak/Nature Focus,
p. 12 (bottom); Pavel German/Nature Focus, pp. 4, 5 (bottom), 29 (right); Peter Marsack/Lochman
Transparencies, p. 10 (bottom); Steve Wilson/Nature Focus, pp. 14 (top and bottom), 25 (bottom);
Stuart Humphrys/Nature Focus, p. 16 (bottom); Wade Hughes/Lochman Transparencies, p. 29 (left).

Contents

Glossary words

When a word is printed in **bold** you can look up its meaning in the Glossary on page 31.

What are flies?

Flies are insects. Insects belong to a large group of animals called invertebrates. An invertebrate is an animal with no backbone. Instead of having bones, flies have a hard skin around the outside of their bodies that protects their soft insides.

Flies have:
- six legs
- two wings
- two **antennae**
- two eyes
- a mouth
- many breathing holes on the sides of their bodies.

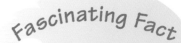

Fascinating Fact

There are at least 150,000 kinds of flies worldwide.

Flies are often brightly colored. This blowfly has a bright green thorax and abdomen and an orange head.

4

What makes flies different from other insects?

Flies have two wings. Other flying insects usually have four wings.

Scientists have given a special name to all flies. They are called **Diptera**.

Most flies are just as clean as other insects. This march fly is busy cleaning its **mouthparts**.

Did you know?

Mosquitoes are flies.

Not all mosquitoes feed on human blood. Some feed only on other mammals, frogs or reptiles. Some do not even feed on blood. This large mosquito feeds on plant sap.

Fly bodies

The body of an adult fly is divided into three segments. These segments are called the head, the **thorax** and the **abdomen**.

Adult flies have hairs and bristles all over their bodies, including around their mouths. These bristles have many different shapes and sizes. They can be long or short, thick or thin. Different bristles have different names. The shortest ones are called pile and the largest are called spines.

Abdomen

The abdomen is where:
- food is digested
- females produce eggs
- males produce **sperm**
- some breathing holes are.

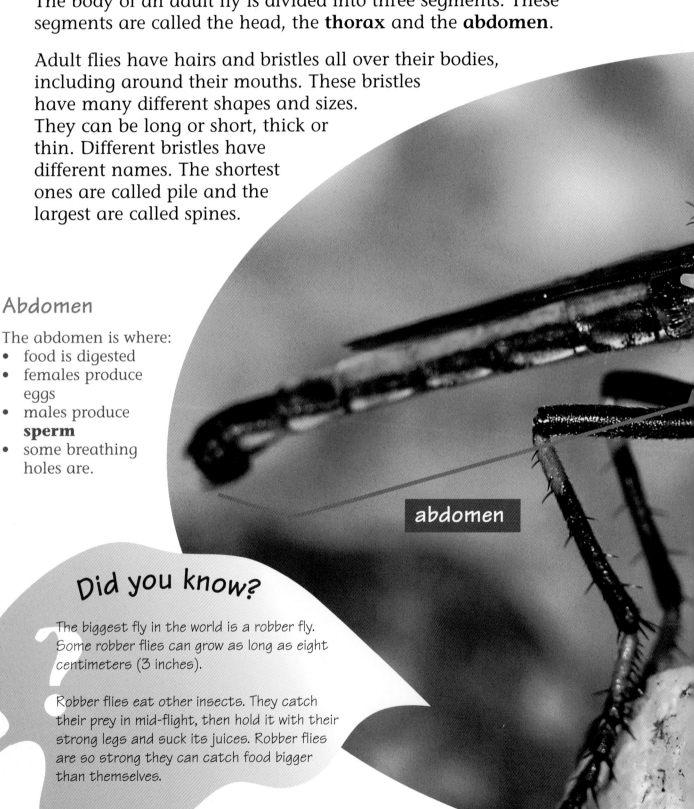

abdomen

Did you know?

The biggest fly in the world is a robber fly. Some robber flies can grow as long as eight centimeters (3 inches).

Robber flies eat other insects. They catch their prey in mid-flight, then hold it with their strong legs and suck its juices. Robber flies are so strong they can catch food bigger than themselves.

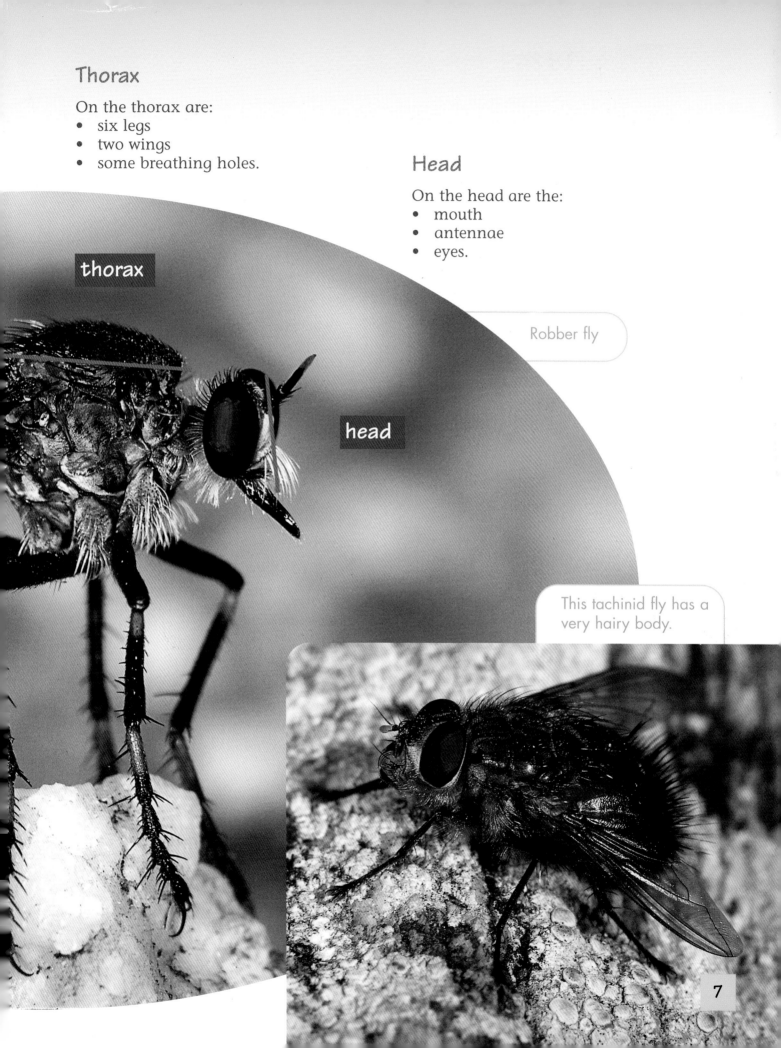

Thorax

On the thorax are:
- six legs
- two wings
- some breathing holes.

Head

On the head are the:
- mouth
- antennae
- eyes.

thorax

head

Robber fly

This tachinid fly has a very hairy body.

7

The head

On the head of an adult fly are the mouth, eyes and antennae.

Mouth

The mouth of a fly is not always the same. What kind of mouth a fly has depends on what food it eats. Flies that suck blood have a hard and sharp **proboscis**. Flies that feed on rotting animals or plants have a sponge-like proboscis. Flies have special mouthparts to help them feel and eat their food. These mouthparts are like fingers so it is as if they have hands at the opening of their mouths.

Eyes

Flies have **compound eyes**. This means that each eye is made up of lots of tiny eyes packed together. Most flies have big compound eyes.

Antennae

Flies use their antennae to feel and smell their environment. Their antennae can be many different shapes and sizes. Male mosquitoes have big, feathery antennae. Crane flies have comb-like antennae.

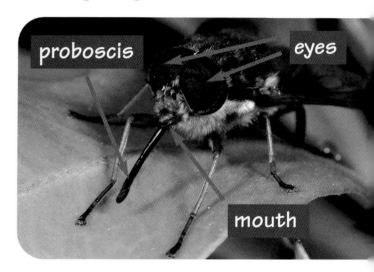

Flies can extend their proboscis out or pull it back in. Sometimes proboscises are soft, and expand and collapse like a balloon, and sometimes they are hard and stay rigid. This march fly has its hard proboscis extended all the way out.

This soldier fly has very simple and straight antennae.

This photo of a fly's face has been taken with a special microscope called a **scanning electron microscope**. You can see the little individual eyes that combine together to make up two big compound eyes. You can also see the fly's antennae sticking straight out between the eyes. The fly's proboscis is extended downwards.

The thorax

On the thorax of an adult fly are the legs, wings and some of the breathing holes.

Legs

Flies use their legs for landing, walking, cleaning themselves and holding their prey. Male flies use their legs to hold females when they are mating. Most flies have claws on the end of their legs.

Wings

Flies have two wings. Each wing contains a network of hard veins. The veins support the wings so they can be used for flying. The veins in different kinds of flies form different patterns. These patterns are always the same in the same kinds of flies. Scientists use these different patterns to identify different kinds of flies.

This is a crane fly in flight. You can see that its wings and legs are attached to the segment of its body called the thorax. If you look closely at this fly you can also see one of the halteres just behind its wing. It is very short, is orange in color and has a black knob at the end.

Flies also have two undeveloped 'wings' on their thorax. These are called **halteres**. Halteres look like short stalks with little knobs on the end. There is one on each side of the fly just behind the wing. While flying, the halteres go up and down. When the wing goes up, the haltere goes down and when the wing goes down, the haltere goes up. Only flies have halteres.

Fascinating Fact

The sound a blowfly or mosquito makes when it is flying is made by the beating of its wings.

Breathing holes

Flies breathe through tiny holes in the sides of their bodies called **spiracles**. Flies do not breathe through their mouths.

Where do flies live and what do they eat?

Flies can live just about anywhere, from the tropics to very cold places, from rainforests to deserts, from mountains to the coast. Flies can travel large distances. They are often found in large numbers near their food.

Flies eat liquid foods such as:
- plant sap and fruit juice
- rotting animals and plants
- blood
- tiny creatures that live in water
- animal waste.

Many flies smell their food. That is how they find it.

This tabanid fly is feeding on the nectar of a peppermint flower.

This robber fly has captured a honey bee. Robber flies are so big and strong that they can even capture dangerous insects like bees.

Fruit flies

Fruit flies make fruit rot. The adult fruit fly lays her eggs on unripe fruit. This infects the fruit with a **fungus** that causes it to rot. When the **larvae** (young flies) hatch, they eat the rotten fruit. The fruit fly is a serious pest for farmers.

Blood-sucking flies

One kind of fly that feeds on human blood is the mosquito. Only adult female mosquitoes suck blood. Males feed from plants. Australia has more than 350 kinds of mosquitoes. Only a few of these feed on people. Mosquitoes find us by smelling the **carbon dioxide** that we give off through our skin and when we breathe. Some mosquitoes like to suck blood from our feet and some like our hands.

Sandflies and march flies also suck blood. Hoverflies drink the nectar of flowers.

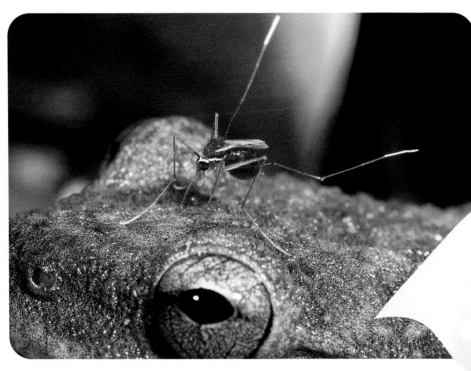

Most mosquitoes get their blood meals from warm-blooded animals like people. Some will feed on **amphibians** like this frog. Some kinds of mosquitoes put their hind legs up when they feed.

Did you know?

Some mosquitoes are dangerous. In certain parts of the world mosquitoes carry diseases such as malaria and Ross River fever. Mosquitoes can infect us with these diseases when they suck our blood.

House flies

House flies are familiar to people because they often come into our houses. They like to live on moist, filthy things outside. When they come inside, they can spread diseases. House flies also like many of the foods in our kitchens.

Flies of different kinds have been attracted to some partly digested meat. Certain kinds of flies like to eat and lay their eggs in dead animals or rotting meat.

Flies that live in deserts and dry habitats

Some flies can live in very hot and dry places like deserts. Here are some of the flies that can live in hot, dry places.

Flies find shelter from the hot midday sun. This is one way that flies that live in hot, dry areas avoid drying out.

This tachinid fly can live in dry places. These flies lay their eggs on other insects. When the **maggots** hatch, they will live inside the body of the other insect. These are big flies with a wingspan of nearly three centimeters (one inch).

In dry areas, flies are attracted to moist things because they are a source of food and water.

These flies live in the desert. These two are mating.

This fly is sitting on the flower stalk of a plant called a grasstree. Grasstrees can grow in dry areas. Many kinds of flies are attracted to the flower stalks of grasstrees because they are a good source of nectar.

Flies that live in forests and wet habitats

Lots of flies like to live in forests. Here are some of the flies that live in forests and wet places.

This is a banana-stalk fly. It lives in the ends of cut banana branches and other rotting vegetable matter. These flies live in warm tropical areas. They have a long, flat head.

Papaya fruit flies live in tropical areas. They are a big pest for fruit farmers. The flies lay their eggs in the fruit and this causes the fruit to rot. These flies are brightly colored and grow to over one centimeter (0.39 inch) in length.

Mosquitoes like to live in wet areas. This female mosquito is feeding on blood. You can see that the sucking part of the mosquito's proboscis is straight and has gone into the person like a needle. The guiding part of the proboscis is bent next to it.

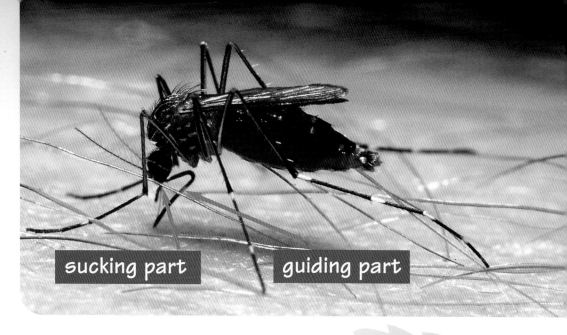

sucking part   guiding part

Flies come in many different shapes and sizes. This stilt-legged fly has very long legs. These flies live in forests. Their maggots live in decaying wood and vegetation.

This small fly lives in forests. It probably breeds in the forest leaf litter.

How flies communicate and explore their world

Flies can get information about the environment in a number of ways. They can smell, feel and see. Flies are usually active during the day but they are often attracted to lights at night.

All flies have compound eyes that can see shape, movement, distance, color and light and dark.

All flies have antennae that they use to pick up smells from food or other flies. They do this by sensing the special chemicals that food or other flies give off. They can also use their antennae to feel their way around the environment.

Flies use their hairs to feel surfaces and objects. Flies also feel sounds.

Did you know?

Flies can taste with their feet. This is because there are special sensors on the feet of flies that detect the chemicals in food, just like the taste buds on human tongues.

Flies get information about their environment through the various bristles on their bodies. They also have good eyesight.

Flies can taste their food as they walk across it. This house fly is feeding on a piece of meat.

How flies communicate

Flies can communicate in a number of ways. They can:
- vibrate their wings to make a buzzing sound
- give off smells
- dance or move around one another
- come into contact with each other by swarming together in a particular place
- stand close together and touch one another.

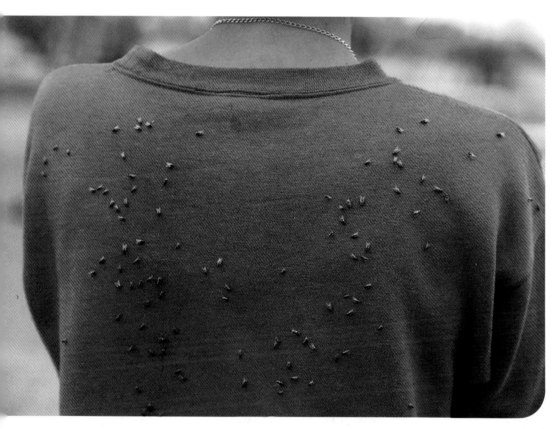

Flies often come into contact with one another by being attracted to the same place. These bush flies have all been attracted to this person's back.

These are the most common flies in Australia. They like grassy areas and lawns. They rarely fly around your face, sit on your back or come indoors, but they can be attracted in their thousands to lights on a summer's night. These flies are harmless and are only about three millimeters (0.12 inch) long.

The life cycle of flies

The whole life cycle of a fly, from egg to adult, can take a few weeks or as long as a whole year. Flies usually lay many eggs. Some lay only a few and some lay larvae.

Flies reproduce **sexually**. This means that a male and a female are needed to make new flies. The male fly provides sperm while the female fly provides eggs. The eggs and sperm need to join together for a new fly to start growing. Males and females find each other by being attracted to the same places. This can be on a piece of dung, a toadstool, a flower, a dead animal, under a fruit tree — it all depends on what kind of fly it is. Sometimes the female attracts the male by giving off special smells.

A pair of flies mating.

The adult eventually emerges from the pupa. When the fly becomes an adult, it does not grow any more. Most adult flies only live for a few weeks.

An adult fly

Fascinating Fact

In one kind of fly, the female's eggs hatch inside her body. The larvae then start feeding on her. She is eaten alive by her growing larvae.

The female lays one or many eggs, depending on what kind of fly it is. The eggs hatch into little larvae that are often called maggots. The eggs are laid near or in food so that when they hatch, the maggots will have food to eat. The female of some flies will keep the eggs inside her body. The eggs hatch in her body and she lays live maggots straight onto the food.

Newly hatched maggots feeding.

The little larvae spend their lives eating and growing bigger. As they grow, their skin becomes very tight until it splits. This allows the larvae to grow even bigger in their new, larger skin. This is called **molting** and it happens several times during the life of a larva.

These are older maggots that have grown big.

The last molt of the larva is special. This is because when the last larval skin splits open, the larva is wearing a soft pupal skin underneath. As the soft pupal skin gradually hardens the larva becomes a pupa. In the **pupal stage**, they stay very still and do not eat — they are turning into adult flies. Mosquito **pupae** are different — they can move about and swim through water.

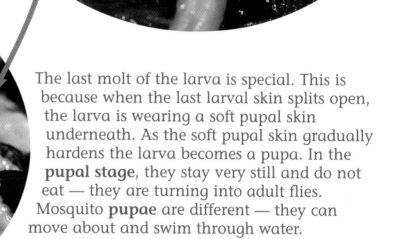

Maggots turning into pupae. As the pupae get older they get darker in color.

19

Maggots

The maggots of flies all look very similar and it is almost impossible to tell what sort of fly a maggot will become.

Maggots have bodies that are like long, white sausages with hard hooks at one end. The hooks are like teeth and they use them to chew through food.

When a maggot is ready to turn into a pupa, it will often jump or skip away from its food. This makes it difficult for insect predators to find and eat them. This is because a single fly pupa is harder to find than, say, a pile of rotting fruit.

This is a bush fly maggot. You can see its insides through its skin. Most maggots are pointy at the front end and rounded at the other end.

Did you know?

Maggots do not have heads. Maggot bodies are much simpler than the bodies of adult flies.

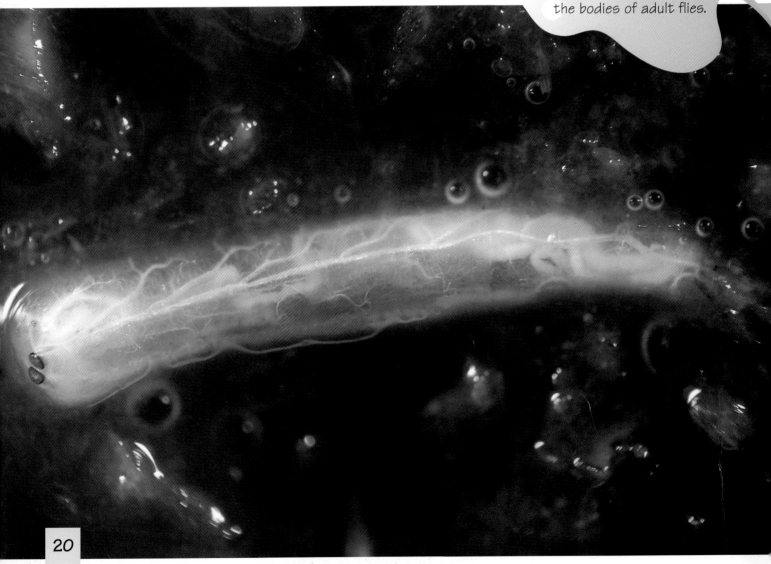

What do maggots eat?

Different kinds of fly maggots eat different foods.

- Maggots usually eat rotting plants and animals.
- The maggots of house flies eat moist, filthy rubbish and horse manure.
- There are fly maggots that feed only on the dead flesh of living animals.
- The metallic-green sheep fly lays its eggs on the wet wool around a sheep's bottom. When the maggots hatch they eat into the skin of the sheep. This can sometimes make the sheep so sick that it dies. This is one reason why farmers cut off sheep's tails.
- Some maggots, like mosquito larvae, live in water. They eat little plants and animals that live in the water. Mosquito larvae are called wrigglers because of the way they move through water by wriggling, then resting. The larvae of different kinds of mosquito wriggle in different ways and rest at different angles.

Did you know?

When fruit rots under a tree, the maggots of different kinds of fly will eat the food in different ways and at different times. Some maggots like to feed on the fruit when it first starts to rot. Other maggots like to wait until the fruit is really putrid.

Green sheep blowfly maggots live in and feed on dung. Like all maggots, they do not have legs.

This maggot was found living in the water inside a pitcher plant.

Mosquito larvae, or wrigglers, swim by wriggling their bodies.

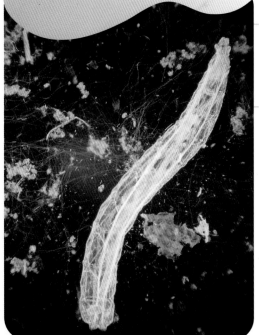

Predators and defenses

When flies are larvae, they can be eaten by other insects or other larvae.

When flies are adults, they are often eaten by other insects. They are also eaten by spiders, bats, birds, frogs and lizards. Sometimes they are trapped in fly-catching plants like sticky sundews, pitcher plants or venus flytraps.

This adult fly is infested with **mites**. The mites weaken the fly and make flight difficult.

A centipede devours a march fly.

Spiders often catch flies in their webs. This spider's web is full of crane flies.

How flies protect themselves

When flies are larvae, they can defend themselves by:
- living in large numbers so that they are less likely to be the one eaten
- seeking out dark places
- jumping or crawling away from their food when it is time to turn into a pupa.

Adult flies defend themselves by being very fast at flying away. They can also protect themselves by looking like dangerous insects.

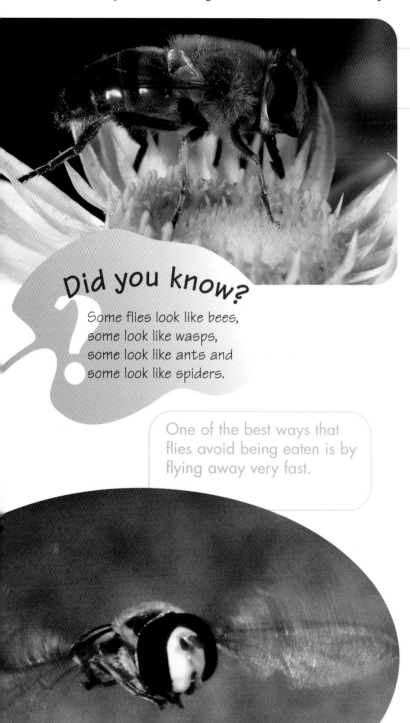

This fly looks just like a bee.

This fly looks just like an ant. It has no wings.

Did you know?

Some flies look like bees, some look like wasps, some look like ants and some look like spiders.

One of the best ways that flies avoid being eaten is by flying away very fast.

Weird and wonderful flies

Welcome to the wonderful world of bizarre and extraordinary flies!

A fly in disguise

This nycteribiid fly looks like a spider. It has no wings and only lives in the fur of bats. It feeds by sucking the bat's blood. This fly has strong claws on the end of its legs that it uses to hold onto the bat's fur. These flies can run very fast, like a spider, across the fur of bats and then disappear by burrowing into the bat's fur. These flies look very strange because they appear to have no head.

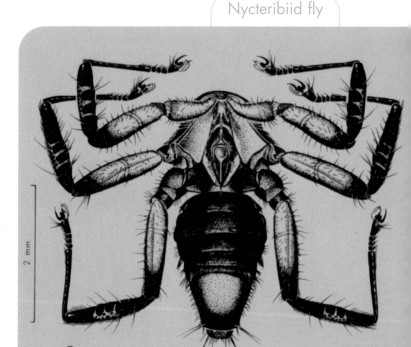

Nycteribiid fly

2 mm

B

Flies with antlers

Some flies can be weakened but not killed by a kind of fungus. Part of this fungus can grow out of the fly's head and it looks like antlers or horns.

Sheep botflies

The female sheep botfly allows her eggs to hatch inside her. She then deposits her young larvae around sheep's nostrils. The larvae crawl inside the nose and grow by feeding on the sheep's blood. When they are mature, the sheep sneezes them out onto the ground. In some countries people can be infected by this type of fly if it gets in their eyes.

Did you know?

Adult flies cannot bite because they have no jaws, and they cannot sting because they have no stinger.

Tsetse flies

The tsetse fly from Africa is a very unusual insect. This is because the adult does all the feeding. The single larva grows inside the female until it gets very big. When she lays it, it does not eat. Instead, it immediately turns into a pupa and then an adult.

Long-legged crane flies

Crane flies look like giant mosquitoes and have very long legs. These legs break off very easily. Crane flies can be found in the corners of sheds or caves and look like daddy-long-leg spiders shaking in the wind.

Stalk-eyed flies

Stalk-eyed flies get their name from the fact that their eyes are on the end of long stalks. There are different kinds of stalk-eyed flies and they live in rainforests.

Crane fly

Stalk-eyed fly

Collecting and identifying flies

There are so many kinds of flies that scientists are still discovering many new kinds. If a scientist catches a fly that is unknown, it is named and described so other scientists can study it too.

When scientists collect flies, they use special equipment. They sometimes use traps, lures or a light to attract flies, nets to catch them with and containers to put them in.

The flies in collections are sometimes pinned or glued to a piece of card. Flies kept this way last longer because they do not bump around in containers. Dead flies do not rot away. They simply dry out and the hard skin keeps its shape.

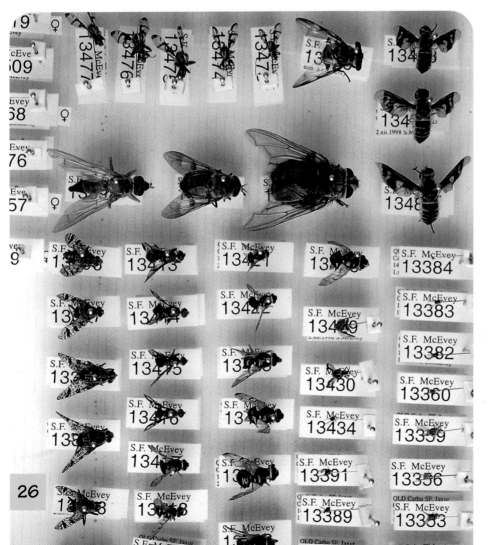

One of the ways scientists catch flies is to get a plastic soft-drink bottle, cut it in half and put the top half upside down into the bottom half. They put bait, like banana or meat, in the bottom half to attract the flies. When the flies go inside, they get trapped.

A collection of pinned flies. The pin gives the scientist something to hold onto when they want to look closely at the fly.

How are flies identified?

Flies are identified by looking very carefully at their shape, size and color. If a fly's shape, size and color is different to all other flies that scientists already know, then this fly is considered a new kind of fly and is given a scientific name.

Fascinating Fact

One of the things that scientists look at to help them identify a fly is the size of the hairs and bristles on the fly and the direction that they point or bend.

A scientist studying flies. An example of each kind of fly that has been found is kept in collections at museums.

What do scientists study about flies?

After a fly has been given a name, scientists then study:
- where it lives
- what it eats
- when in its life cycle it is a pupa
- how often it molts
- what makes it turn into a pupa or an adult
- what are its natural predators
- what poisons or pollutants kill it or interfere with its normal life cycle
- what diseases it carries
- what chemicals can stop it flying.

Ways to see flies

We are surrounded by flies but rarely take any notice of them. Here are some ways that you can look more closely at them.

- Have a look at the tiny insects around a light. Most of these insects will be little flies.

- Look in spiders' webs. What flies can you recognize?

- Swing a butterfly net over some flowers and then see what insects you have caught. Look out for angry bees!

- Swing the net over rotting vegetables on a compost heap. Put the net on the ground and carefully put a jar and a lid inside to trap the insects. Are these flies different to the ones you caught on the flowers?

- Swing the net over some long grass. These flies will be different again.

This fruit fly has been attracted to a piece of fruit.

Observing flies in summer

Squash a rotten banana in a dish and leave it on a classroom table. Make sure that it is summer but do not leave the dish in the sun or in a strong breeze.

See what insects are attracted to it overnight. Tiny ferment flies will probably be the first visitors, often within a couple of hours. These are little orange flies with red eyes. They will have found the banana by smelling it.

After several days, there might be a swarm of these flies and you might even see their larvae burrowing in the rotten fruit.

Try leaving out different foods and see what kinds of flies are attracted to them.

- What flies are attracted to a piece of rotting meat?
- What flies are attracted to rotting fruit?
- What flies are attracted to rotting (not drying) mushrooms?
- What flies are attracted into the kitchen in summer when a roast dinner is in the oven?
- What flies are attracted to rotting cucumber?
- What flies are buzzing around the window in the classroom?
- What flies are attracted to a veranda light at night?

This fly has been attracted to a piece of bread.

This flesh fly has been attracted to rotting meat.

Flies quiz

1   How many wings do flies have?

2   How do flies breathe?

3   What is the scientific name for flies?

4   Are mosquitoes flies?

5   Do male mosquitoes suck blood?

6   What kind of flies are the biggest flies?

7   Do all flies lay eggs?

8   Where are a fly's halteres?

9   How do many flies find their food?

10   What are maggots?

11   What are mosquito larvae called?

12   Why do some flies look like insects that sting or bite?

13   How many different kinds of flies are there in Australia?

14   Are most flies clean?

15   What sort of eyes do flies have?

Check your answers on page 32.

Hoverflies feed on flower nectar. See if you can find this hovering fly around a flowerbed.

Glossary

abdomen	The rear section of the body of an animal.
amphibian	A kind of animal that has a backbone and that can live on land or in water (like frogs).
antennae	The two 'feelers' on an insect's head that are used to feel and smell. (Antennae = more than one antenna.)
carbon dioxide	A gas given off by living things.
compound eyes	Eyes that are made up of many tiny eyes packed together.
Diptera	The scientific name for flies.
fungus	Mushrooms and toadstools are kinds of fungus. Some fungi grow flat on or under the skin of animals. (Fungi = more than one fungus.)
halteres	Knobs or stumps that were once the second pair of wings on flies.
larvae	Caterpillars, grubs and maggots are kinds of larvae. In the life cycle of an insect the larval stage is after the egg stage and before the pupal stage. Larvae hatch out of eggs, grow and then turn into pupae. (Larvae = more than one larva.)
maggots	Fly larvae.
mites	Small spider-like animals that are not insects.
molting	When an animal sheds its entire skin it molts. The process is called molting.
mouthparts	Structures around the mouth that help an animal handle its food.
proboscis	A long thin mouthpart used for feeding.
pupae	In the life cycle of insects (like moths, beetles and flies) larvae turn into pupae. Adult insects later emerge from pupae. A cocoon is a shell around a pupa. (Pupae = more than one pupa.)
pupal stage	A stage in the life cycle of an insect when the insect is a pupa.
scanning electron microscope	A type of camera that makes photographs with electrons instead of light. It is used to take photos of the smallest things.
sexual reproduction	When a male and a female living thing combine to make more living things.
sperm	The male reproductive cell.
spiracle	A tiny breathing hole in the side of a spider's or an insect's body.
thorax	The middle section of an animal's body.

Index

Answers to quiz

1 two 2 through holes in the sides of their bodies called spiracles 3 Diptera 4 yes 5 no 6 robber flies 7 no 8 on its thorax behind its wings 9 they smell it 10 fly larvae 11 wrigglers 12 to protect themselves from predators 13 at least 7,000 14 yes 15 compound eyes.